CARVER
A Great Soul

WISE AS SERPENTS   HARMLESS AS DOVES

Fairfax, California

CARVER
A Great Soul

Peter Duncan Burchard

6-20-99
Washington, D.C.

To Bob and Molly Freeman,
In the Spirit that
guided George Washington
Carver!

Peter Duncan Burchard

Book design by Kate Henke Design, Oakland, California
Cover design by Peter D. Burchard, Sr. & Kate Henke
Cover photo: Carver, age 38, holding a clump of soil, Tuskegee Institute,
1902. Library of Congress.
This book is printed on recycled paper.

I dedicate this to the elders who
have taught me much and helped me with this work:

Norah G. Porter (1903-1996)
>   Dear Norah listened to my drafts in prose.
>   While turning it into verse I felt her spirit
>   so lyrical and loving, like a muse.

Jason Lotterhand (1911-1997)
>   Great Jason, for whom Carver long had been
>   a hero, had me read to him and Jean,
>   his wife, a draft the *Oklahoma Eagle*
>   had printed. Rarely does an author have
>   such listeners. That was my last sight of him.

Ethel Edwards (1916-1997)
>   Friend Ethel gave me all the help she could.
>   She was the author of a book on Carver,
>   written with valuable assistance from
>   Jim Hardwick, one of Carver's closest friends.

Jeanne Goodwin, born in nineteen hundred three:
>   a woman who, I thank the Lord, has stayed
>   among her loved ones long enough to see
>   these firstfruits of my work with Carver, whom
>   she met and saw so clearly.
>   Her presence at the center of this project
>   with energy, appreciation, insights,
>   and critical alerts to blindnesses,
>   has placed me in her throng of grateful students
>   and made this work so much more real and true.

A restful man sat steeped in silent thought
aboard a train that crossed the rolling Ozarks.
Here he'd been born and raised, in days before
the rails had reached Missouri's southwest corner.
His frame was spare, his shoulders somewhat stooped
from lifelong habit. He was sixty-three.
Passing so close to where he'd grown 'til ten
brought back his boyhood in near-virgin forests
and prairie; wading in the limestone springs
with minnows in the sun and frogs for friends.
In youth he had received the gift of wisdom.
He heard the voice from nature's holy heart—
the small, still sound of the Creator's counsel.

The hills and draws resounded with the rattle
of railroad's rhythmic clatter on the tracks
as George Washington Carver thought of Jim,
his loving brother, who had long since died.
Jim had been all the kin he'd ever known
after the terror of their mother's loss.
She'd been the slave of Moses Carver. George
had been an infant when slave raiders rode

on horseback to the cabin. They had found
young Mary clutching bundled baby George.
They'd kidnapped both. George was returned alone,
near dead. Her owner showed his love for Mary
by giving for her son a racehorse worth,
in 1865, three hundred dollars.
Moses and Susan Carver, German settlers,
had, nine years earlier, accepted Mary
as payment of a debt. They had been kind.
After they lost her, though both up in years,
they'd raised her sons as theirs. George learned of Mary
through Susan Carver's tears.

The boys then knew no other of their people.
On rare trips to Neosho, they'd seen blacks.
Twice yearly Mose had driven his horse-drawn cart
eight miles to small Neosho to have grains
he'd grown ground into flour and buy supplies
like sugar and molasses. Either Jim
or George accompanied friendly Mose each time.
At home they'd made their soap, spun wool and flax,
and gathered wild spring greens for food and medicine.
The little George, frail-bodied but in mind
so quick, had questioned constantly the works
of wondrous nature in those Ozark wilds:
What made them? And what might he then create?

Now, passing through the night, George Carver's steaming train
screeched slowly to a stop with steely sounds
into Neosho. Here, when he was ten,
he'd walked alone to enter school—his first
except for one which he and Jim soon left
after enduring cruel ridicule
for differences in skin.
His train sat in Neosho quite a while.
He did not leave his seat nor did his friend.
Turning his head toward the quiet night,

2

*Carver with
some of the
amaryllis he
bred for nearly
fifty years.*

he tried to see the outlines of the town
to which he'd come on foot from Carver's farm—
not knowing where he'd stay, looking for work,
a soul so thirsty for an education:
at ten, a child intent on finding answers.

The answers were within the eyes that saw
his face reflected in the train car window.
His eyes contained reflections of the flowers
from everywhere he'd been, and trees and hills
and animals—birds, insects, forest creatures—
and skies and eyes of all humanity.

They mirrored all the joys and tragedies
of life on earth. The setting of his sights
on nature's glorious beauties, kept the joy
predominating in his deep-set eyes.
Each creature told him of our Maker. Through
all nature's forms, George Carver spoke to God.
The heaven the Great Creator showed to him
through every living thing was evident,
to those who saw past surfaces to souls—
in gentle eyes, alive and wide awake.
His vision spied the milk-and-honey land
where folks observe the Golden Rule and do
to others as we'd have them do to us.
The features of his face appeared well-carved
and smoothly curved as creek bed stones. His skin,
deep brown, was dark like earth's most fertile soil.
His nose, a downward arrow, pointed past
a straight-line mouth that often bent in smiles.
Deep creases crossed his forehead in broad waves
adapting easily to looks of hope,
of study, or of happiness. His forehead
soared somehow to infinity above—
infinity within.

N ot interested in his image, Carver
leaned closer to the window for a view
into Neosho's station and beyond.
At ten o'clock p.m., the moon just down,
it was too dark to recognize a thing.
In memory he met Mariah Watkins.
The boy he'd been, on reaching town, had found
the school for blacks. In need of rest he'd crept
into a barn next door. For several nights
he'd slept there. Then one morning before dawn
Mariah Watkins found the timid child—
a stutterer, and every inch a farm boy:

*Mariah
Watkins of
Neosho,
Missouri.*

coarse brogans, jeans, plain shirt and hat of straw.
Within a little bundle he had folded
his earthly goods, his whole inheritance—
his only book, an extra homespun shirt,
outdated magazines, his favorite rocks.
Mariah Watkins was the region's midwife,
herbalist, trusted family nurse and doctor.
She was a queenly and commanding woman

with Indian features. She was sanctified,
and danced the way the holy people do.
She'd questioned George out in her barn and then
as mothers in the tribes of Africa
have done from time beyond remembering,
stretched out a wing and given him a home.
She and her husband, in their twenties, had
been slaves into their teens for no more reason
than having ancestors from Africa.

George would have had a welcome at the Carvers'
if he'd returned to stay. He never did.
He'd visited now and then from towns in Kansas
where he had worked his way through primary
and high schools. Once a joyful George told home folks
of his acceptance to a Kansas college.
They later heard that on arrival there
he had been turned away for his complexion.
Two decades after that, he'd come to see
Moses, high in his nineties. By that time
he was a full-fledged scientist and Professor—
still wearing brogans, calm as an old shoe—
talking to God through flowers and hearing Him.
He'd stopped in at the Watkins' on that visit.
Mariah saw that her advice to George,
to serve their people, had become his calling.
A neighbor, one of George's former schoolmates,
dropped by in horse-drawn buggy, looking smart
in livery. Cal Jefferson recalled,
"Seeing George with all his brains and me with none
and all dressed up, it made me feel ashamed."

Mariah had lived 'til 1925,
two years before the train now carrying George
en route to Tulsa, brought him through Neosho.
His mental record of how long he'd lived there

was lost. Nine months? Two years? He wasn't sure.
His memories of his painful past—his years
of drifting in pursuit of schooling like
a swimmer in a storm grasping a raft—
stayed wrapped in darkness like that moonless night.

Fifteen more miles of track and he was in
the state of Oklahoma. Here his train
rolled off the Ozark Plateau towards the plains.
While still within the Ozark's lowly foothills
he reached the Frisco Station in the midst
of Tulsa and its ninety thousand souls.
The population thirty years before
had been a thousand settlers living in
a muddy little horse-and-buggy town.
By riding high on Oklahoma's boom
as oil wells gushed and money flooded in,
Tulsa had spread like waters from the river
by which it stood—the Arkansas, swelling
above its low banks. Like ignited oil
it had burst out into a bustling city.
His train pulled in just minutes after midnight,
October fifth of 1927,
the first of four days of a Negro Fair.
The Negro Fair Association hoped
that George Washington Carver's presence there
would be a drawing card. They had been thrilled
when he'd agreed to come a thousand miles
bringing his famous products made from peanuts—
soap, shaving lotion, wood stains, dyes for cloth,
milk, candles, coffee, powder for the face,
linoleum, axle grease, massage oil, cheese,
stock food, bleach, tan remover, paper, wallboard.
His product count was then two hundred two.

Harry O. Abbott, right, on his third and last long tour with Carver, second from left, in early 1930, at the Topeka, Kansas home of Dr. and Mrs. Marvin and Cora Ross.

With Carver on the train was Harry Abbott,
his traveling secretary from Tuskegee,
an Institute for blacks in Alabama.
Booker T. Washington had built the school
with students digging local clay for bricks,
then raising campus buildings. Carver had
worked nineteen years with charismatic Booker,
instructing students and the local farmers.
He'd stayed on since the dynamo had died
twelve more years, so his work in agriculture
and chemistry would serve their hard-pressed people.
Abbott had been just two years at Tuskegee
in charge of teaching printing, but the school
supported his accompanying Carver
who, after thirty years of hauling boxes
and making his own plans, could well use help.
Friend Harry, serious and businesslike,
was there for three long journeys, two to Tulsa,

of which this was the first. To him George Carver wrote:
"You not only relieved me of every responsibility
connected with the trip but was always on the alert
and seemed especially happy when you could add
anything to my personal comfort, which I appre-
ciate far more than I have words to express."

And Harry wrote to Carver:
"...you are more than chemist, botanist, mycologist,
scientist, creator... you are indeed a "master of things."
And far above that... you are a prophet, a seer, a man
among men, and truly a man of God. And to me,
since I made that first Oklahoma trip in October 1927
with you, it has been the man side, the human side
of you that has appealed to me. I grant without
question all the appraisals of your scientific
accomplishment, but all that pales into insignificance
when compared with your magnificent stature as a
simple, loveable, kind-hearted soul, whose very
presence is a benediction and whose interest is a
blessing."

They stood to leave the train. Both were tall,
a little over six feet. Abbott wore
a pleasant, earnest gaze beneath a forehead
quite prominent and high. At thirty-eight
he was still fit to lug the boxes which
he wrestled off the luggage rack. He dressed
in fashion—suit and tie, fedora, oxfords
and woolen overcoat.
Waiting to greet them on the platform and
escort them to where they would stay in Tulsa
was Mr. Hooker, owner of a store
in partnership with Carver's Tulsa host.

Compared to Harry and to Mr. Hooker,
George Carver was distinctly individual.
The little country boy was with him still,
the boy who never learned to dress for show,

who valued what's within humanity
above appearances.
His jacket and his pants were not a match.
The jacket at the sleeves was frayed with age.
His shoes looked old. His cap was of the kind
that cabbies and the newsboys used to wear—
extended in the front, snapped to the bill.
He dressed so that he would not have to change
when he went out to study God in nature.
His women friends among Tuskegee's teachers

who taught domestic handicrafts and skills,
though very fond of him, would often tease him
about his ways so thoroughly countrified—
tried to humiliate him into neatness.
And though he loved them, he would feign annoyance
and tell them, "If you want to see fine clothes
I have a trunkful of them in my room."
A sculptor carved his bust, and friends asked what
he thought. He answered them, "I don't know how
I look. It's never interested me."
In Carver's seeing eyes, a person's skin
was just another layer of their clothing.
To him, each human soul was interesting
and worthy of respect. His studies of
the countless species nature emanates
showed ours most wonderful and strange, and dangerous.
He prayed we would express our kinder side
and kept a watchful lookout for the good.
Being black in the United States—the country
so tardy to let go of slavery—
he was reminded many times a day
that dark complexions were regarded as
a badge of badness, as if skin could make
a man inferior.
America's besetting sin, its weakness,
was everywhere apparent then in Tulsa,
America's most segregated city.
From Tulsa's Frisco tracks, three "men of color"
had only one direction they would go,
and that was to the north.

They walked by waiting rooms marked "white" and "colored"
to Mr. Hooker's car, then drove a mile
to Tulsa's northern edge. They reached the home
of James and Carlie Goodwin, in their fifties.
Their house was perched above the street, upon

*James
Henry and
Carlie
Goodwin's
home on
Haskell
Street
where
Carver
stayed.*

Thanks to Jeanne Goodwin.

a gently sloping hillside. It had been
just recently completed. They had owned
another home until six years before,
when in the Tulsa riot, theirs had been
one of the thousand houses lost in flames.
With constant work and James's canny sense
for business, they again had their own home.
The careful keeper of the house was known
as "Sister Carlie." She was motherly,
rounded and dark-complected. Some judged James
as white. His forbears mostly were Caucasian.
Their son Ed's wife once commented on this:
"When people talk to me about 'your people'
I say, 'Which of my people do you mean?
The Irish, African or Jewish ones?'"
If you should read this in a wiser time
when people judge each other not by skin
or judge each other not at all but look
into the eyes for souls, you well may wonder:
"How strange, these Negro fairs and strict divisions
of cities in such arbitrary ways!
It must have been a dark age in those days."

Their hostess led them through the dining room
and then a hall, into a quiet bedroom,

12

its furniture mahogany, carved with roses.
Leaving their luggage they returned to say
good night to Mr. Hooker and to thank him.
Then Hooker and the Goodwins, with amazement
informed their visitors of an invitation
from Tulsa's all-white School Board.
The superintendent had expressed a wish
that George Washington Carver come address them.
They'd never heard of such a thing in Tulsa.

But Harry knew the power of the man
who always wore a flower in his lapel.
His language was the clear one nature teaches
which reaches hearts and hearers of all kinds.
People would shed their shallow racial notions
when in the presence of a soul so wise,
and love him for himself.
His songlike voice at first was a surprise,
so high-pitched was his clear and carrying speech.
This may have been the effect of scars left on
his throat from whooping cough, resulting from
exposure to the cold, that night when raiders
had stolen infant George with mother Mary.

*Carlie and
James Henry
Goodwin*

The hour now late—or early—they retired.
Carver would customarily arise
at cockcrow on the farm and wander out
to walk in God's cathedral, known as nature.
He'd talk to Him and listen, gathering peace
and quiet to his soul. He'd meet the creatures
invisible at other times of day.
This morning, having been awake 'til one
and being in an unfamiliar city—
he must have missed his walk, a rare event.
He'd find a time before the day was spent.

At breakfast, Carver learned the Goodwins' story.
They were from Mississippi. James had worked
on railroads, Carlie in their people's schools.
The schools in Mississippi for the folks
called "colored," didn't go beyond sixth grade.
For their four children, James and Carlie wanted
more education than their state afforded
so, fifteen years before, they'd sojourned west
to Tulsa, whose black schools had given all four
the keys to colleges. The main school in
North Tulsa bore the name of one whom Carver
had known and loved, Booker T. Washington.
Their schools were built and kept with cash that flowed
from oil three hundred million years in age,
which derricks drew from subterranean pools
across the river, several miles southward.
There in the river's bend Tulsans had built
refineries. Their city had become
a hub for oil flowing through buried pipelines
all over Oklahoma. The hard-timers
who sought new life close by the booming strikes,
and Pennsylvania oilmen, had been joined
by families like the Goodwins, seeking schooling—
an educational opportunity
for children of a people long oppressed.

Elders instilled in young folks diligence
and aims to excel, to help their people's progress,
lifting their hopes up—even while aware
of having to work twice as hard as whites
for half the gain. Carver, who'd worked through school
alone, from ages ten to thirty-two
came to embody, for some striving students,
a strength in knowledge and in selfless service.

Carver had noticed from his bedroom window
an easy slope, still open to the sky.
While Harry took directions to the fairgrounds,
Carver walked out into the warming morning
to have a wider view of Standpipe Hill,
which he intended later to explore.

The fairgrounds were at Tulsa's southeast edge.
The way to them was through the all-white section.
North Tulsa's streets were treeless. Blacks had built
their town anew but trees had not grown back
since Tulsa's night and day of deadly fire—
to some, the worst of racial riots ever.
As Carver watched the sudden southward shift
from treelessness to trees he traced the story.

B ack in the years when he'd been growing up
on Mose's farm a hundred miles away
from where today the town of Tulsa stands,
the city's site was in its virgin state,
a sea of grass that seemed unending westward.
The storms that swept unchecked across the plains
unleashed their coils of lightning, sometimes catching
a towering grassy sea afire and with it
burned out invasive sprouts of woody species,
allowing native grass to keep its hold.
The blackened plains sprung back in brilliant green,
regenerated by the purging flames.

The only trees surviving prairie fires
were oaks and willows by the riverbanks.

Where Tulsa is, a little settlement
of Creeks lived by the river in their huts
of sticks and mud. They'd dwelt in Georgia's forests
and Alabama, 'til the people came
whom they called "sycamores," their skin being tinted
like whitish bark on trees. The "sycamores"
had driven the Creeks out to the treeless tracts
at that time called the Indian Territory
and later to be known as Oklahoma.
The railroad tracks being built from east to west
brought "sycamores," at first a trickle—settlers
who came to use the land for grazing herds
of cattle. Claiming properties, they'd stopped
the cleansing prairie fires at new-drawn boundaries,
so woody brush began to build. Their stock
left native grasses trampled which allowed
their alien grains brought in on trains to gain
a foothold and invade the open spaces.
Then they had found the oil near Red Fork hamlet,
a pool so vast in value and in volume
for men depending on its use in engines.
Just two years later, Oklahoma's statehood
began when Tulsa's stores supplying oil wells
had whiskey flowing free from kegs. Some wild ones,
drink-filled, fired guns in air to add to noise
of singing, yelling, whistles, bells, parades.

While Tulsa grew its grid of tree-lined streets,
even up until the time of Carver's visit,
an Indian still owning land would be
visited by a white man who would tempt him
to drink fire water from his flagon. Then,

weakened by drink, the Indian signed a paper,
not comprehending that he'd lost his land
with that one little motion of his hand.

I n Tulsa's mushrooming and change appears
a microcosm of the nation's changes—
the separation of its peoples and
the white man's often ruthless rush for riches
in forms of land and minerals and oil.
Such alienation and such reckless haste
disfigure life's great universal weaving.
The threads had already been tangled by
the time some whites burned all North Tulsa down.
Carver addressed these ills—their source and ends.
He found the underlying cause of all
our troubles in the hells that we create.
He taught his Bible students at Tuskegee:
> "[I] heard a person say, 'There goes a fellow in a living
> hell.' This can be true. We make our own hell or
> heaven. We bring upon ourselves little moments of
> hell when we think and act a little meanly toward a
> fellow student or a fellow American, black or white.
> When our thoughts—which bring actions—are filled
> with hate against anyone, Negro or white, we are in
> a living hell. That is as real as hell will ever be. While
> hate for our fellow man puts us in a living hell,
> holding good thoughts for them brings us an opposite
> state of living, one of happiness, success, peace. We
> are then in heaven."

George Carver prophesied a shift from use
of resources which earth has formed through ages,
epochs, periods and eras, to the ones
that we can grow within a single season.
He gazed beyond the day of industries
which, we've since learned, are killing animals
and plants with whom we've shared our odyssey,

and now we'll see no more. In Carver's words:
   "I believe the Great Creator has put ores and oil on
   this earth to give us a breathing spell... As we exhaust
   them, we must be prepared to fall back on our farms,
   which is God's true storehouse and can never be
   exhausted. For we can learn to synthesize materials
   for every human need from the things that grow."

The kind of industry George Carver had
   within himself—carved in his character—
had shown since he was young. He'd yearned to learn
to make things with his hands. At many crafts
he'd been a brilliant scholar. He had kept
a thriving garden everywhere he'd settled:
Neosho and in several towns in Kansas.
After he'd been rejected by the college
for his complexion, he had moved out west
and taken up a claim and built a home of sod
among the ranches so remote and lonely.
He'd learned to paint and studied holy nature,
so when he moved to Winterset in Iowa
a woman used her influence to help him
into a college, where he studied art.
At Simpson College, he at last had felt
he was a human being.
The gentle man, then in his early twenties,
inspired the white girls in his art class with
his diligence, his purity of heart,
and his belief that flowers like those he wore—
the stars of earth—were messengers of God.
He sang a glorious tenor or yet higher,
played the accordion, fiddle and guitar
and he could whisper reveries on piano.
At Ames in Iowa studying agriculture
he'd earned, by 1896, his Master's.
Booker T. Washington had heard of him
and called him south to teach both young and old:

to treat the land with compost, plow it deep,
grow their own food, make things, avoid the store—
the program Carver titled "Live at Home."
He daily read the Bible which he taught
to young men at Tuskegee. As a chemist
developing his Protean Product Show
he'd labored from before daybreak past nightfall,
a steady habit bringing happiness.
His peanut demonstration gave to those
who studied it this message which George Carver
had worked so steadily to tell the farmers:
"The peanut as a legume or a pea
enriches soil from air—draws nitrogen
to nodes upon its roots. Do all you can
to build back up the worn-out soil. The land
that people waste will leave the people wasted.
For peanuts you are growing in Oklahoma
here are two hundred two suggested uses.
In everything that grows, great good resides
for those attuned to knowledge God provides."

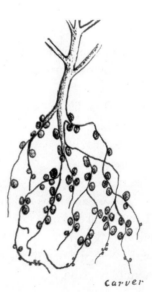

carver

*Carver's
drawing of
the nitrogen-
bearing
nodules on
legume roots,
from his
1910
Tuskegee
bulletin
promoting
the growing
of cowpeas,
or black-eyed
peas.*

Their car rolled onto Tulsa's spacious fairgrounds
at half past ten, three hours from opening.
The carnival was ready. Khaki tents
defined a midway but the place was quiet.
The empty livestock barns had, one week prior,
housed cattle for a state fair held by whites.
In stables, horses were being groomed to race
that afternoon or run through paces in
the evening rodeo.
Carver and Harry found the roomy hall
for home exhibits where housewives and farmers
arranged arrays of robust seed and produce,
canned goods, cookies and pies.
Harry located space for setting up.
Carver's display was rows of labeled bottles
showing what man can find in just one plant.
The products were in place by half past three.
The turnout still was low, and they were tired.
They drove back to the Goodwins', took some rest,
and then, as day's high heat began to fall,
walked out to answer Standpipe Hill's soft call.

George Carver loved the lofty verse from Psalms
saying, "I will lift mine eyes unto the hills
whence comes my help." By looking far to hills,
he understood our human aspirations
to oneness with the Lord of all that lives.
Walking upon their slopes, he found the healing
in medicines from roots and leaves and seeds.
Standpipe was grassy as it long had been,
beyond ancestral memories of the Osage—
who'd lived the longest in that Great Plains region.
Now, here and there, a tree had taken hold:
the oak that twists to spread its branches wide
and bears their weight with dense and fibrous wood
or a persimmon, then in fruit but green.

On Moses Carver's farm, the sweet persimmons
were Jim and George's favorite Christmas candy.

On Standpipe Hill one might expect to see
a standpipe at the top, but it was gone.
The city's water by that time was held
atop another hill. Carver had come
to study plant life and geology.
The sandstones and the clays there overlay
the limestone George had known back in the Ozarks
through creeks and caves he played in. Here, below
the uplift, those same limestone layers were buried

down where the oils of ancient forests pooled.
Some of the plants upon the hill revived
his early memories of Missouri's herbs
and some had spread there in the interim,
becoming common. In them all, he saw
the virtues placed there by the Great Creator.
He found the plantain: leaves for bee stings, seeds
in clusters which contain a mucilage,
a gentle laxative for the intestines;
the dandelion: its root a liver tonic,
its leaves, to eaters of spring greens, a medicine.

For Carver, food and medicines were one.
The steady medicine of healthful food
was how from frail youth he'd grown strong and well,
for decades at a stretch avoiding illness.
He had the keys of health, both physical
and mental, as he fed his mind on beauty
so marvelously made, delighting in
God's great creation story.
A magazine for children heard from him:
> "To me, my dear young friends, nature in its varied
> forms are the little windows through which God
> permits me to commune with Him, and to see much
> of His glory, majesty, and power by simply lifting the
> curtain and looking in."

On Standpipe Hill he talked to God and heard Him.
It was his sanctuary there in Tulsa,
his refuge from the loudness of false life.

Since Carver walked on Standpipe Hill, the noise
of human lives has amplified. Today
one there can hear the din from multitudes
of engines, still consuming ancient oil
on barren asphalt plains, their roar and smell
unsettling health and peace of all that lives.

Harry once said that when he drove his car
with Carver as his passenger, his friend
would ask him please to stop beside the road.
He'd glimpsed a plant uncommon in those parts
or else a fungus strange in its effect
and wanted time to study it more closely.
George Carver's eye for fungus growths is rare
for anyone at any time on earth.
Mycologists, out on a stroll with him,
were awed when he would spot a species which
'til then had not been sighted in the state.
Poor farmers out in rural Alabama

Carver
examining
trees along
the Long
Island
Expressway
during a trip
to New
York and
Michigan in
late 1939.

23

and those who wrote to him of blighting fungi
were benefited from his wealth of knowledge.
Harry, when Carver asked, was always happy
to brake his car and turn the motor off.
He'd watch a master naturalist at work,
who lived, not pent in ghoulish atmospheres
nor in the thoughts of abstract theories—
but touched real life, communed with it, and loved.

Since Carver studied Standpipe Hill, it has
been overgrown with woody vegetation.
Brush now hides refugees from rushing worlds
which have no home for them—where they are crushed
who do not move so quickly, as on highways
where speedy steel mobiles will kill the slow.
The lesson in George Carver's lifelong work
can guide our way to real prosperity
for all at the expense of no one's needs.
He pointed past the age of war-forged iron
by giving his friend Henry Ford ideas
on plastics from the farm. Ford's "soybean car"
anticipated ones to come—lightweights
which sip their fuel, their loads being so reduced.
Through Carver's time in Tulsa, we may catch
his vision, like a gem inwardly lit.
We'll look at facets through the fair's four days,
then see him home, and finally return
to Tulsa as he dedicates a school,
the largest of the many named for him.
There's much to learn from him and here no hurry,
which he has taught me and I bring to you.
Like walking through a field with him, we'll pause
as if we stopped to wonder in a flower.
Here, like visiting bees, we'll drink his words.
His teachings help us to expand beyond

the tiny circles in which we have bound
ourselves, like larvae of the butterflies.
Meeting him in a segregated oil town
gives us a glimpse of woes that kill us still—
like poisonings of our God-made bodies, and
analogous pollutions of the mind
(by actions like the Klan's displays of hate
when they burned crosses up on Standpipe Hill).
In some of Tulsa's citizens we'll find
the love and wonder of a world more kind.

Earlier, when Carver's hostess heard where he
was walking, she had told him of a brick plant
which he and Harry found by going east.
Then from the pit, with long and tapering fingers,
he pulled a lump of clay and studied it.
The knowledge came to him of many uses
aside from bricks, like pottery and paints.
He'd made these things from clays back home to show
the poor folks how to cheer their humble homes.

In minerals, as in the things that move,
he found the life and mind of his Creator.
The year before this trip to Tulsa, Carver
had spoken in Virginia, and impressed
a young white man who recognized his depth,
and wrote to ask how he might gain such knowledge.
Carver responded:
> "Begin at once to study nature, both animate and
> inanimate. One must know plants, minerals, birds,
> insects, animals, in fact the more one knows about
> the things God has created, the better he can talk to
> Him."

Carver's suggestion that we can commune
with God through forms which many see as lifeless,
is echoed in another letter to
a young Virginian in whom Carver's friendship

25

had melted race disdain. He wrote to him:
> "I do love the things God has created, both animate
> and inanimate. As He speaks aloud through both."

The sunset guided them back to the Goodwins'
where after one of Carlie's well-cooked meals
they drove back to the fair. Around George Carver
convened a friendly cluster of his people.
To farmers and to all, he spoke and listened,
learning from them conditions of their soil.
They peppered him with questions. Every one
he answered well and wisely. It seemed he knew all things!
South Tulsa's paper carried this report:
> "What the opening hours... lacked in exhibits and
> crowds... was made up by the enthusiasm [and] the
> quality of products shown... Holding the spotlight
> was an arrangement of 202 different products of
> peanuts, all worked out in the agricultural laboratory
> at Tuskegee Institute by Dr. George W. Carver."

*Truman
A. Penney
of Tulsa.*

Tulsa Historical Society

As Tulsa's fairgrounds opened Thursday morning,
Carver found someone waiting hopefully
for him—a portly, balding, friendly white man.
George Carver, after thirty years and one

remembered T. A. Penney as his friend.
Penney awakened memories of Ames,
the agriculture school on Iowa prairie—
all white except for George when they'd been there.
Penney's favorite was of a competition
in oratory, in which both had entered.
The night before, Penney had sought out Carver,
whom he could trust for kind encouragement.
He'd climbed the ladder to his attic room
and tried his speech on him. George calmed his fears
of failure. When the contest time arrived
and Penney stepped up to the podium,
his nervousness returned. He looked to George
whose eyes brought back to mind, "I know you can.
You'll do just fine." And he succeeded well.
Then Carver, the engaging speaker, who
while in his teens had overcome his stutter—
captured the crowd, the judges, and the prize.
For two full hours the men caught up—conversed
of Penney's chain of drug stores there in Tulsa,
while Carver, never in a hurry, made
his old friend laugh with his bright bits of humor.

The President of Tulsa's Negro Fair,
    named Amos Hall, responding to the failure
to draw the hoped-for crowds, decided to
eliminate the fair's admission cost.
Most of the folks they wanted to attract
were far from rich. Only a few had made
their fortunes off the oil wells, very few.
Blacks mostly labored in refineries
or worked as live-in nannies and domestics
in homes of whites. Such household servants were
the only blacks south of the Frisco tracks
after the sun had set.

North Tulsans, by financial standards of
their people, had done well.
The Greenwood Business District was well-known.
"The Negro Wall Street" was its other name.
A visitor from the Negro Business League
before the riot thought of Monte Carlo.
The riot ruined many. They'd rebuilt,
restored their city to prosperity,
but many still saw tickets to a fair
as unaffordable.

For workers in white Tulsa, Thursday was
their day off. Heading home to see their families
they made the northern section so alive.
Now with the price impediment removed
of entry to the fair, North Tulsans ventured
southward, streamed in the gates and down the midway
where barkers called from booths, "Come win a doll!"
Cold drinks sold in the heat. The people went
to view the projects that the youths had made
in black schools there and in surrounding counties.
Carver saw people of the Osage tribe
and Cherokees, and those who showed a blend
of African and Indian. Cherokees,
before they'd been pushed west from Southern states
had traded with the whites for slaves, who then
became like members of their families.
Fair president Amos Hall had welcomed whites
by telling a reporter:
> "We especially invite the white people to attend this
> fair, that they may see what the black race has been
> doing with the educational facilities offered them."

The empty livestock barns had filled with fowl—
Rhode Island Red, Barred Rock and Leghorn chickens.
The great and lofty-ceilinged hall where Carver

had his exhibit, with its floors all strewn
with straw, both loose and still bound up in bales,
now sang with lively voices.
The vacant spaces had been filled by farmers
and housewives showing how to live at home.
In quiet homes, the spirit may be strengthened
as we produce the things we need ourselves.
People may feel more peace and need less business.
Our busyness is working where we live—
industrious, but free of industry
where masses, trapped in herdlike work for moguls,
move strangely far astray from who they are.
The program "Live at Home" which Carver preached
there at the Negro Fair was on display.

*Carver,
around age
fifty, with
vegetables
and fruits
he had
preserved.*

B ack at the Goodwins' home that evening, Carver
was ready when two men—the principals
of Tulsa's black schools, came to pick him up.
Tall, pleasant Mr. Woods of Booker T.
was one whose voice was law among his staff.
From Dunbar, Mr. Hughes, a young mid-fifties,
was held in high regard among their people.
They drove him to that meeting which caused awe
in all who heard that whites had asked a black
to come and speak to them.
Even these days, Tulsans hearing of that night—
historians and the older longtime residents
like white Ruth Avery, then in junior high—
call it anomalous, unusual.

Ruth Avery, as the seven-year-old Ruth Sigler,
was witness to the worst. Six years before
George Carver walked on Standpipe Hill, Ruth sat
on that same hill and watched North Tulsa burn.
She saw a plane fly over, dropping bombs
on fine Mt. Zion Church, which faithful Baptists
had raised, finishing just six weeks before.
Nearby, white men, dressed in their uniforms
from what we know as World War One, then recent,
had brought machine guns, which they aimed below.
Ruth Avery said, "Blacks knew about the whites
by caring for their children, homes and food.
My nanny was a black and Cherokee.
But whites knew almost nothing of the blacks.
They knew young blacks had fought in World War One
so they could handle guns. They were afraid.
My uncle took me up on Standpipe Hill,
as he had heard that northwards from Muskogee
some blacks were marching to defend their own.
This it turned out was true, but they were stopped
outside of town." Ms. Avery's observation

*Ruth Sigler
(later Avery),
Easter, 1921,
about a month
before she
witnessed the
Tulsa riot.*

on fear in whites of what they did not know,
was Carver's theme when he would quote this verse:
    "If I knew you and you knew me—
        and if both of us could clearly see
        with an inner sight divine
        the meaning of your heart and mine,
        I am sure we would differ less
        and clasp our hands in friendliness
        if I knew you and you knew me."

But Tulsa on that fearful night in May
of 1921 witnessed a war
between the citizens of one same nation.
The Frisco Station's walls were scarred with bullets

as black men who had served in World War One
defending the U. S., where they were born,
had to protect themselves against the people
of their own native land.
White men had plundered every store in town
that dealt in guns; and then they set North Tulsa
aflame. Hundreds of people died that night.
The whites turned auditoriums in town
into internment camps for blacks they'd captured
while homes the blacks had worked to build and keep
went up in smoke and down to ashy ground:
because a young shoe-shining man, allowed
to use an elevator in South Tulsa
stepped on a woman's foot; because she screamed
and said she was attacked; because, although
the whole thing could be heard by many people
and though the cops could see no cause to book him
until next day, a paper picked it up,
their pages hurling words like "lynch" and "nigger"
out to the frightened whites who thronged the space
outside the courthouse jail; because young blacks,
a little group, approached the crowd with guns
like those the whites had also brought with them;
because a white man asked insultingly,
of one of them, why he had brought a gun
and he replied, "To use it if I need to;"
because a white man struck, erupting Tulsa.

All these "becauses" help us not at all
to know the cause. When people harbor hate
in hearts; when they reject the antidote
of unifying love for all God's creatures—
the pain of fear-fed hate turns to abuse,
the seeming nearby cause a mere excuse.

This history may help us understand
amazement of the Tulsans then and now

on hearing of that night when Carver crossed
the Frisco tracks by special invitation.
No written law existed to prevent
the Superintendent of the Tulsa schools
from asking George Washington Carver to
their meeting, but it simply was not done.
A code not often drafted into statutes
but one the whites upheld in spite of this
was, "If we fear or feel a threat, we strike."

P rincipals Woods and Hughes showed Carver to
the meeting room where they with Harry Abbott
were four black men among a mass of whites.
The board and school officials had been joined
by some of Tulsa's high-placed civic leaders.
And Harry wrote that Superintendent Claxton—
a tall and well-built man with jet-black hair—
while introducing Carver, which he did
in well-delivered speech, spoke beautifully.
Harry then wrote:
> "For more than an hour the gathering listened
> unusually attentively to the address of Dr. Carver, at
> the close of which he privileged them to ask
> questions. This they did and were marvelously
> enlightened on many things."

To win his crowd George Carver did not need
to play the fawning smiler. He would find
in all the eyes the souls of those he saw.
He spotted instantly the ones who had
creative minds and real intelligence—
more wise than smart, the spiritual ones,
receivers of creative power from God.
He turned their thoughts to nature's ways. That night,
he spoke of the persimmon trees he'd seen
whose fruit is often wasted, and he said
the fruit could easily be dried and saved

to cheer cold winter days.
To shun political and racial themes
he did not have to be a hypocrite.
"I am a scientist," he said. "I haven't time
to spend on things so far outside my field."
But every day reminders of his "race"
were thrust into his way unpleasantly
and so, inevitably, he spoke of it.
When he'd been at Tuskegee seventeen years
in 1913 he had this to say:

> "...there is no question or questions peculiar to the
> Negro, but simply a problem of humanity; and the
> same methods of procedure which have worked such
> wonders in the civilization and evangelization of all
> other races and peoples, are equally applicable to the
> Negro. Why not? He is moved by the same impulses;
> he responds to joy, grief, disappointment, failure,
> success, etc. exactly the same as other people in like
> circumstances."

George Carver's conquest of a crowd of whites
by simply being himself, he'd done before.
The young men whom he called his "Blue Ridge Boys,"
religious men of their Y.M.C.A.'s,
from shock at Carver's presence at a conference
in Blue Ridge, North Carolina, were turned round.
They had become disciples; looked to him
as to a loving father, to a teacher.
They'd set up tours to all-white colleges
for what he called his interracial work.
At Southern colleges, he spoke from rostrums
where no one black had ever stood before.
He'd captivated students who from birth
were trained to keep their people separate:
to have the blacks defer to them, tip hats,
step off into the gutter of the street
so they could pass, use separate restaurants
and rest rooms, trains, schools, all facilities.

As Carver later wrote to Dr. Claxton:
>"I have had some very unusual meetings in places
>where there was considerable doubt as to just how I
>would be received on account of my color. Strange
>to say, I got my largest and most appreciative
>audiences in those places."

Of Carver's time in Tulsa, Harry wrote:
>"In my opinion Dr. Carver's visit did much to create
>still further interest in the welfare of the colored
>people of Tulsa on the part of the whites, who are far
>more kindly disposed than the unfortunate affair of
>1921 would indicate."

Harry, in conversation with the President
of Tulsa's School Board, asked that he arrange
a tour of a refinery for Carver.
He answered that he would, for Saturday.
During the drive back north, Principal Hughes
invited Carver to the Dunbar School.

The next day, Friday—third day of the fair—
George Carver rose when he awoke, at four.
He walked up Standpipe Hill to watch the light
arriving, and to keep his contact clear
with God, to maintain strength and mental presence
throughout the day. He said of all his walks:
>"I put off the finite, put away every material problem
>and then you are given a glimpse in the Infinite and
>its secrets are revealed."

That morning he took note of all the plants
that yielded medicines, and counted them.
He prayed that he could teach effectively
the lessons that the plants had taught to him.

Principal Hughes of Dunbar Elementary
came by soon after breakfast, as arranged,
and drove him to the school. Carver inspected
the classrooms and the cafeteria.

He was delighted with their children's garden.
Professor Hughes, so mightily impressed
by Carver's speech the night before told students
what Carver meant to him, as Harry wrote:
> "...using Dr. Carver as a living vitalizing example,
> Mr. Hughes drove home some telling points into the
> hearts and minds of the upper class, impressing upon
> them in an indisputable manner the possibilities and
> opportunities that are open to boys and girls of vision,
> adding that color need be no barrier in so many
> avenues of life and offering Dr. Carver as a crowning
> illustration of the part."

When children heard George Carver's voice, they wondered.
They looked up as he touched the mysteries
of spiders, snakes and worms, insects and flowers.
He'd tell of reaching out each day for knowledge
in loving all of God's creative works.
This man so harmless and so kind, they felt
was open to them, not trapped in himself.
If they had read or heard that he'd been born
a slave, and of his wandering, working search
for schooling, often meeting bars in ways
of progress, then they knew he understood.
Their struggles for a moment felt less heavy
with this strange scientist who did not grope
but spoke from certainty, awakening hope.

The Dunbar School librarian that year
had filled the window sills with crowds of flowers
in pots. This woman, Jobie Holderness,
then twenty-seven—told, at ninety-five,
a story of a student at the school,
a future minister. She helped him learn
to love the flowers and cherish simple life.
The preacher he'd become brought bright bouquets
of cheer to her, out of his thriving garden.
That is the kind of minister that Carver

Jobie E. Holderness, master's graduate in library science, about ten years after she saw Carver on his tour of the Dunbar School.

believed could have the best effect on folks—
ones bringing messages from the Creator,
that nature is so eager still to teach.
The knowledge Mrs. Holderness passed on
was of the kind which Carver knew brings out
our true humanity. With it, we rise
to our best selves and fill our destined place
with creativity—true children of
the Great Creator God, living in happiness.
Carver was pleased to see the artistry
deep in each human soul, find its expression.

To him, a farmer working near to nature
in rich, clean soil, his tools in good repair
was artful; so were cooks preparing food
nutritious and appealing, and the women
sewing their clothes, and using things at hand
to make what's needed. Carver's ideal school
would have a greenhouse like the one he saw
at Dunbar, from which students took home slips
of vegetables and flowers. Their teachers went
to check on how they'd helped their plants to grow.

Paul Laurence Dunbar, namesake of the school
George Carver visited that chilly morning,
had spent a fine spring day visiting Tuskegee.
It then was Booker T.'s domain, and Booker
had asked Dunbar, a poet, for a poem.
His words became Tuskegee's anthem song:
    "The fields smile to greet us, the forests are glad.
     The ring of the anvil and hoe
     Have a music as thrilling and sweet as a harp
     Which Thou taught us to hear and to know."

Such joyful meeting of life's basic needs
as instruments of God, was Carver's way.
He never lost his touch with finer things
like those which Dunbar wrote of in this couplet:
    "Because I've loved so deeply and so long
     God in His great compassion gave me song."

That day at Tulsa's fairgrounds, nearly all
who'd heard him speak the previous evening came
to see the peanut products of the man
who'd won their hearts, and question and converse.
This crowd included also seventeen students
from rural Claremore's black high school—a group
comprised of all the juniors and the seniors.
The principal escorted them to see

Paralee "Pal"
Coleman
about two
years after
she saw
Carver at the
Negro Fair.

exhibits and enjoy the carnival.
They rode the merry-go-round and the canoe
that rocked them, leaving some folks feeling queasy.
Among the junior girls was Paralee,
called "Pal," who emanated innocent
and friendly strength. At ninety, she recalled:
"People who didn't know him thought they'd see
a man well-dressed with deep, commanding voice.
But all his audience accepted him.
You couldn't get close to him for the whites."

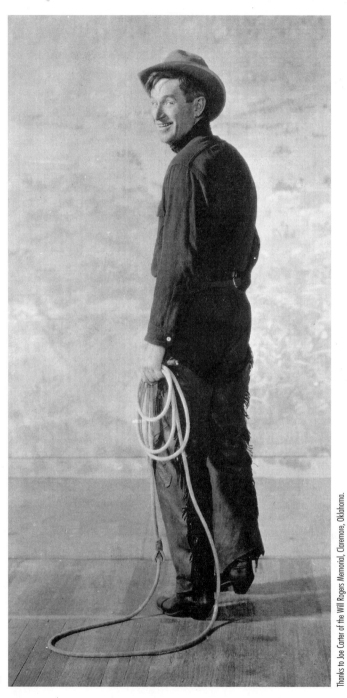

Will Rogers

George Carver was like someone else from Claremore
whom he would meet just five months after this—
Will Rogers. Gentle Will was he who said,
"I never met a man I didn't like."
The crack-smiled soul made rooms roar with his humor.
His lariat tricks, first shown him by a black man,
were famous nationwide.
He teased the high and mighty of his day
and loved them all, and saw beyond the skin.
Since Paralee had been a little girl
she had adored him, knowing he would bring
his friendliness and presents for the young
when he returned, renowned worldwide, to town.
Will Rogers (Cherokee and European)
and Carver (possibly pure African)
throughout all ages are among the greatest
in hearts of love for all humanity.
Will would acknowledge Carver as the greater.
While on the speaking tour which took him near
Tuskegee, he stopped by to see the school.
He looked through Carver's laboratory with him.
Then, after Sunday service in the chapel
Will Rogers spoke to all the congregants,
mostly of Carver. He then turned to him
and told him, "I wish it were possible
for me to spend at least three weeks and sit
at your feet as a pupil."

That evening George Washington Carver went
to an insurance building in North Tulsa
with rooms capacious for a dinner crowd
for Dr. Carver's speech.
That was what Harry called him, as did many
who knew that he could doctor anything
in plant or animal kingdoms, and with men
help body, mind and soul—strengthening faith

as surely as the robed divinities.
In forests he found herbs to doctor herds,
compounding powders to condition cows.
He was a master doctor of the soil—
the dust of eons, filled with little lives
which thrive as much on human loving kindness
as so-called higher creatures.
So, mineral, vegetable and animal
and those who fed a heavenly aspiration
found profit in the Doctor's wise prescriptions.
The first time anyone had called him doctor
was back when he was quite a tiny boy.
The housewives in the region of the farm
where he was raised, would bring him sickly plants.
It was a mystery to them what he did.
He took their plants out to his secret garden
hid in a woodsy space and talked to them
and sang to them. One thing those women knew—
that little stuttering boy on Carver's farm,
the shy young Negro boy, could doctor plants
as well as anyone.

In compensating for his lack of school
'til ten—struggling, alone and self-supporting—
he had, by thirty-two, far more than earned
his Master's. For the work that he had done
to go that far, if he'd been white, he might
have held by then a doctorate or more.
Carver deserved his honorary name.
Within a year of that October evening,
the Iowa College where he'd studied art
conferred on him an honorary doctorate.
This pleased him, because Carver hoped that all
his work would be a credit to his people.
For this same reason he had never left
Tuskegee Institute, though many times
the job had tested limits of endurance.

Once Thomas Edison had asked if Carver
would come and work in his New Jersey lab,
for pay which might have made him rich, but Carver
would not consider going where his work
would not be known as his—and would not cast
a positive reflection on his people.

That Friday night he stood among his people—
a three-piece-suited crowd of lawyers, doctors,
clothiers and druggists, owners of cafes,
a hotel, nightclubs, movie houses, dress shops,
a newspaper and general stores and groceries.
After the riot, several of their lawyers
had fought the all-white city government
as they maneuvered legally to steal
North Tulsa for their own commercial use.
By real estate appraisals and an ordinance
to tighten city codes, they tried to stop
the blacks from building back their homes and shops.
But Carver's audience through force of will
and friendly generous cooperation
had raised their second thriving town from ashes.
They had to have their own; in all South Tulsa
only one rest room was for them to use.
A woman walking south of Archer Street
across the Frisco tracks to buy a hat
was made to pay before she tried it on.

Carver well understood their history
and circumstances. Most of them had left
the rural South. The dangers they had dodged
of being dispossessed by wily whites
were ones which Carver had anticipated
for people who abandoned Southern farms
for urban scenes—New Orleans, Harlem, Tulsa,
Chicago and Detroit.
He'd warned them that they ran towards a trap,

telling them, "If you have a patch of land
and use your Godly wisdom growing food,
mending the soil, with nature as your tutor,
you might have happiness in peaceful lives.
If we each build a farm, we build our people."
But this was not the way that things had gone.
As slaves and then on tenant farms they'd learned
that farming was less noble than a life
among the softer gentry. This mistake
had held back blacks and whites alike. Most blacks,
perpetually in debt to white landowners,
had filled their fields with the prevailing cash crop,
soil-robbing cotton. Carver had advised them,
"Diversify! Grow food!" They learned too late
the perils of reliance on one crop—
a lesson from the Mexican boll weevil.
As farmers left for cities, Carver feared
that distance from the soil was fraught with dangers.
Our cities rise and fall depending on
conditions of the all-supporting earth—
which, as we heal or hurt, yields wealth or dearth.

S o many of the people there that night
had deep religious feeling. Carver fed this
with passages from Scripture they had heard
and welcomed as he spoke:
    "Where there is no vision, the people perish."

He told them of his early morning walk
on Standpipe Hill and finding herbal cures,
of twenty-seven species growing wild.
Continuing, he said:
    "I found down in Ferguson's Drug Store on North
    Greenwood seven patent medicines containing in
    their formulas elements in these plants on Standpipe
    Hill. The preparations were shipped in from New
    York. They should be shipped in from Standpipe Hill.
    My people are perishing for lack of knowledge."

44

"They murder a child when they tell it to keep out of the dirt. In dirt is life." George Washington Carver.

He reasoned that if people knew the virtues
of plants that they walk over every day,
the economic outcome of his vision
could soon support the people everywhere.

Though Carver prophesied a time beyond
all oil wells, coal mines, mining of all kinds
(instead of hydrocarbons, carbohydrates
as plants supply our every earthly need)—
while whites were pulling profits from petroleum
he told his people they might share the wealth

45

by careful observation of the land:

> "Some day, somewhere, some man is going to say, 'oil is
> here and oil is there,' and oil will be where he lays his
> finger. The whole theory of geological science is going
> to be revolutionized; it just as well be some member of
> this audience who will do this as anyone else."

George Carver forty years before had laid
his finger on an oil deposit, but
had only prophesied someone would find it
and no one had. It stayed beneath the ground
(where it had spent three hundred million years)
'til near his death in 1943.
When it had been unearthed near land which George
had owned in western Kansas, O. L. Lennen—
his former neighbor—told an interviewer
of meeting George, when both were in their twenties:

> "I found him wandering over the country near Beeler.
> He was very interested in scientific subjects even
> then, and on this day he was studying geology. 'Mr.
> Lennen,' he said to me, 'Some time they're going to
> find something under here. I don't know what it will
> be, but I've been all over these hills. There's a big
> dome under here and they'll find something, you
> mark my words.'

> "Well, about a year ago I had the pleasure of sending
> him a plot of the Beeler oil pool. It is just where he
> said it would be more than fifty years ago. It will
> probably take in the old Carver Quarter. If George
> owned it now he could die a rich man. But George
> wouldn't have kept it if he'd known for sure there
> was oil under it. Getting an education was the one
> thing that occupied his mind. He sold that land in
> June, 1891 to go to school."

George Carver's speech in Tulsa was recorded
in Oklahoma City's *Black Dispatch*.
The writer, at this point, observed of Carver:

> "Standing there bent with age, the noted speaker
> and chemist frowned down upon the class of folk

46

who seek truth in shallow places. 'Life requires thorough preparation. Veneer isn't worth anything; we must disabuse our people of the idea that there is a short cut to achievement; we must understand that education after all is nothing more than seeing and understanding relations of one thing to another. First you get an idea about a given thing, then you attempt to drift back to the cause. There is a life study in the attempt to determine the first causes in any given thing.'

"As an illustration of what he meant, Dr. Carver went on to point out that in the study of the sweet potato, one must first understand that a sweet potato was not a potato at all, but belonged to the morning glory family. 'If you did not understand this in the outset, every step you made would be in the wrong direction.'"

This speech of Carver's can acquaint us well
with facets of his deep but simple vision.
He saw that as we classify creations—
seeing plants in families, and human beings
all as a single species—we will come
to recognize the real relations of
all living things, giving a stable basis
to thought. One beneficiary of
these words of Carver's was strong Roscoe Dunjee,

Carver's friend Roscoe Dunjee, the courageous editor of the Black Dispatch, *in 1955.*

the *Black Dispatch's* editor and guide.

He later wrote to Carver:

> "In a large measure you have reorganized my thinking and outlook at life. I especially got a new slant on effective living when I absorbed your idea of education... 'Education is understanding relations.'"

Then Carver—winging, as he always did,
with nothing more than jotted Bible verses,
revealed what science is:

> "Science is truth. A theory is only a theory because it lacks truth. The Bible gives us the best support in this conception when we read, 'Ye shall know the truth and the truth shall set you free,' and then it says in support of application and concentration, 'Study to show thyself approved of God.' Is it not meet and proper that we should make our contribution to civilization?"

With this he urged his people to seek truth
through study of the world we're born into,
as he had done since birth. The information
he had received through everything in nature
had helped to form in him a sage's soul.
He'd found the truest purpose of our lives
in service to the world, neglecting none
in need—serving the whole humanity.
George Carver's life was one of constant service.
For tours he did not charge a penny past
expenses. Pay at home was low. He'd worked
for decades with the poorest, most oppressed
of farmers, who were snared in slavelike systems.
He worked to help dispel their ignorance
and show them how to ease their illnesses
by pointing to the sustenance and uses
of resources they'd overlooked or wasted.
Determined that his science be of use,
immediately, to those in deepest need,

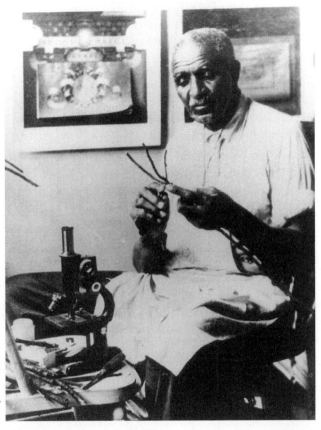

he purposely avoided processes
too technical—keeping his work in reach
of persons farthest down.
Carver believed that science, being a study
of all the creatures God has made and makes,
can't possibly conflict with a religion
of love for all that lives.
If science—seeking what is real, to use
it well—is holy, then the so-called "science"
which leaves the truth of unity to pander
to private gain, casts in its path a slander.

Carver then told of some whom he had seen
who he believed had strayed from real life:

> "I have stood around here at nights since I have been
> here, watching the movements of the young Negroes
> of your city. I have watched them jazzing and dancing
> around. I do not suppose that they are far different
> from the young Negroes in any of our large cities,
> but my thought has been as I looked upon their giddy
> nothingness, 'How much can the world depend on
> you?'"

The people he had seen are like some youths
of any "race" in racing urban worlds.
Distracted from their wonder in what's real,
they have become so dull and distant that
they've lost the thrill of looking into life
and making things themselves.
A woman who lived through the Tulsa riot,
and stayed and built back up her burned-down business,
thought on her town in 1989:

> "Sometimes I think we need a back-to-the-farm
> movement. The black city neighborhoods are dying,
> either in neglect and decay or being scooped up by
> the bulldozers. On the farm we could at least raise
> our children. The cities are overloaded, and the cities
> are not for children. Children need some place to
> grow."

Carver's next words that Friday night touched on
the key to his success, in being just
himself—not trying to be someone else.
He tried to help his hearers to be free
of vision limited by racial thinking
to which he understood they all were tempted,
but someone had to start the mental shift.
He said to them that night:

> "The world is looking for creative minds. Creative
> genius is what makes people respect you. It's not a
> color question, it's a question of whether you have

what the world wants. We can conquer if we will only do it."

The *Dispatch* writer wrote:
"In this connection, the speaker said that following one of his lectures and demonstrations in a Southern city, a white Southerner arose in the audience to make a confession. He said to his white friends, 'I was taught by my father that a colored man never thought independently. He told me that a white child and a Negro child were the same up to their twelfth year, after then the white child began to advance, while the Negro child began to imitate. I want to ask my white friends tonight, who has this Negro imitated?' 'He sat down without another word,' continued Carver, 'and nobody answered his question.'"

Carver went on to say:
"Learn to do common things uncommonly well. We must always keep in mind that anything that helps fill a dinner pail is valuable.

"I saw a plant up on Standpipe Hill that has rubber properties in it. The world is on a search for rubber. Edison and the mighty are looking for a substitute for the present supply upon which the earth now depends. It would be better for your children to learn how to find rubber than to learn some of the other things they are taught in school."

George Carver learned from Thomas Edison
of his research into the rubber plants.
Just four months prior, Edison had written
asking if Carver knew young botanists
whom he could recommend to search the field
for families yielding sticky, milky ooze—
the milkweed, nettle, mulberry and fig
(the family of the Indian rubber tree),
the dogbanes and Euphorbias, or spurges
(the family of Brazilian rubber trees).

Carver then spoke to them of his research:
> "Why, if one just knows the peanut, he can find food and
> shelter, he can produce medicine out of that same peanut,
> washing powders also come, face bleach, candy, boards
> used in the walls of a home."

His search for peanut products had begun
when he was advocating for the soil
by telling farmers, "Plant soil-building peas—
the cowpea or the black-eyed pea, the soybean
and peanuts—not just soil-depleting cotton."
Some farmers had responded, but demand
for peanuts then was almost none at all.
They were for circuses or, in the South,
a tiny patch for children to enjoy.
So Carver thought, "I must increase demand."
Out on his morning walk, he asked of God,
"What is a peanut, and why did you make it?"
He told his crowd these things that Friday night.
His speech before his people ended with
a paraphrase of those same words of Christ
which he had spoken earlier, as he said:
> "You shall know science, and science shall make you free."

And science a la Carver, which is truth,
can free us from our cruel and foolish ways
with nature, prospering our later days.

On Saturday, quite early in the morning,
the weather fair, Carver and Harry crossed
the bridge across the wide and broadening river
growing by tributaries as it flows
from Rocky Mountain streams to Great Plains grandeur.
They drove to offices where they were met
by H. T. Bennett, corporation chemist.
He was to be their guide around the grounds
of a refinery—West Tulsa's largest.
Mid-Continent Corporation blanketed

a thousand acres of the open prairie
with storage tanks and sludge waste ponds, and towers
aflame as they burned excess natural gas.
Excess, though, was to Carver not a word
appropriate for anything from nature
as he worked day by day to save the wastes.
But costs of the extraction of the oil
and moving it to where it will be used
means merchants must move massive quantities
of products to turn profits. Such a process
is wasteful of what does not fit that scheme.
George Carver saw the inevitable end
of drilling and of digging deep in earth
for oil and minerals, as every region
meets all its needs through products from its farms.
Indeed, in early automobile days
the farmers didn't need petroleum.
They ran machines on alcohol distilled
right on their farms from surplus grains or hemp.
But Prohibition had brought Federal agents,
who, claiming farmers might be making booze,
smashed their distilleries.

Their chemist tour guide took the two men to
a huge rectangular enclosure where
the crude oil pouring in from near and far
all underground flowed up, across, and down—
through pipes so wide, into the giant unit.
There workers, black and white alike, walked 'round
on stairs and walkways of step-echoing steel.
Their sounds were drowned by roaring of machines
and whooshing furnaces where crude oil burned
making the steam to fracture other crude
to gasoline, benzine, naphtha—fuels and solvents.
Bennett yelled through the din that every day
they filled more than one hundred railroad cars
with products like the fuel for Model T's

and newer cars—the mounds of molded steel
then coming into style.
The noises with which such gas-burning engines
fill up the world, Carver perceived as threatening
the hearers' health. He commented on this:

> "The type of life that most of us live is not conducive
> to long life and physical strength as the intolerable
> noises and excitement that we are called upon to
> live under at all times breaks down nervous force
> and mental forces also."

Carver, from on the walkway, looked below
at what remained after the fracturing.
Down at the unit's base, an oil sludge pool
collected. It would go to storage ponds
where it just stood, a toxic danger zone.
Bennett told his two visitors, that daily
they turned out six or seven tons of sludge
for which they had no use to profit them.
Carver's keen artist's eyes saw in the sludge
strange colors, like on snake and lizard skins,
where other eyes might only see black goo.
Though some, describing skin like Carver's, say
"oil black," he saw in all our planet's peoples
the many shades and hues.
He thought he might create some useful paints
out of those colors in the sludge below.
It grieved him to see anything be wasted.
In nature's way of life and death, he'd seen
all things are useful. Throwing things away
is deviation from her flexless law
which, heeding, we may live and die content.
Carver related to petroleum
much as he had to cotton—seeing beyond
the day it would be used, but, while it was,
helping avoid the waste. In Alabama
he'd woven cotton stalks into fine mats
to show alternatives to burning them.

*Cotton
stalk mats
hand-
woven by
Carver.*

As he and Harry climbed into the car
for their return to town, he asked if Bennett
might send a jar of sludge to him, to run
some tests on. Bennett said he'd see it done.

C arver and Harry then recrossed the river
to greet the people on the final day
of Oklahoma's second Negro Fair.
They packed up the exhibit, thanked the Goodwins
and rode the tracks back home to Alabama
on trains propelled by burning coal as old
as Oklahoma's oil. Three hundred million
of earthly revolutions 'round the sun
have passed since oil and coal of Pennsylvanian age
were trees and giant ferns and horsetails—woods
so deep and thick, where never mammal walked

nor flower was seen. Then, even dinosaurs
were not yet known to earth. The complex forms
were the amphibious animals emerging
from earth's one-ocean womb and standing pools.
Such forests, wet and lush, grew over much
of what is now America—as if
the primitive plants beside the creeks we know
were magnified; a real primeval world.
Beneath that ancient shading foliage
the plants that died had piled in thick black humus
(according to the wasteless ways of nature
where old and dead still serve to feed the new).
This turned in time to peat, then coal or oil.
The oil in rocky pockets lubricates
the joints within the planet's moving plates.

From Bennett came the sludge to Carver's lab.
There he made iron blue from iron red,
and pretty peacock green, which oxidized
from yellow he had left in open air.
He tested for the heavy metal lead.
Mid-Continent crude was low in asphaltines
and so, it since is known, made lesser paints.
The world that Carver saw ahead avoids
problems like this, of how to use such wastes.
By finding many uses—as he did
with peanuts—in the plants right by our homes,
we may surpass the age of industries
which, for our short-term comfort and convenience
imperil all the good that we have gained.

In Alabama on the vast grand campus
that Booker T. had wrestled to existence,
George Carver was the friendly scientist.
In early mornings, following his walk,

he answered letters. As he once explained:
    "I always sleep over a problem. I never open my mail
    until after supper... I go to sleep with them on my
    mind, and the next morning I see the method and
    the new perspective which usually clears it up. I didn't
    do it. God has only used me to reveal some of His
    wonderful providences."

His correspondence was voluminous.
His letters number some twenty-five thousand.
To follow up a friendly conversation
he'd had with W. F. Graham of Tulsa's School Board,
Carver sent Graham persimmons he had dried,
to show commercial possibilities
of the persimmon tree, reminding Graham
of wealth available at Christmastime—
that cheery orange fruit which George and Jim
as boys preferred to candy.

The original caption for this photo, from 1937, reads "Dr. Geo. W. Carver
reading one of the more than 3,000 letters that he has received relative to his
Peanut Oil treatment for infantile paralysis. The jars and vases in the picture
(upper right) have been made by Dr. Carver from Alabama clays. These
represent only a small part of his experimentation in ceramics."

He also wrote to Superintendent Claxton
of twenty dyes he'd made from green persimmons—
jet black, midnight and English blues, and browns.
In springtime, W. F. Graham wrote this to Carver:
"I wish you had been with me yesterday. I find so
many things in the great out doors I should like to
talk to a master about... Elm trees are beginning to
bud and bird life seems to be very busy finding places
to make their nests. If you will pardon me for
enumerating all these little things, but I know you
love the great out-of-doors, and probably won't
object."

So Carver wrote to him:
"I think it is so delightful to have you enumerate the
things you have. It shows that you are in touch with
nature and nature's God, through which we can
communicate with the Great Creator and learn much
of the creation story."

Graham's letter also said:
"We were up to the farm and late Saturday afternoon
a bevy of twenty or more Bob Whites came up and
ate with the chickens. They were so gentle one could
nearly touch them with their hand."

To this Carver replied:
"How interesting to know that the Bob Whites are
so gentle. I hope that they will remain so. That is
certainly a compliment to you, sir. It is an interesting
truth that animals recognize a kindly disposed
person."

Graham sought advice on poisoning of trees.
Carver wrote back that on Tuskegee's campus
they used an axe to cut around the tree,
a girdle through the bark, then let it die.
George Carver chose the clean old labor way.
They'd made, he wrote, not one experiment
in killing trees with poison.
He added other ways to kill he'd heard—

with coal oil or paradichlorobenzene—
sure death to trees but, as we since have seen,
disease to us, and other creatures who
must feel the terror of our error too.

The government in Tulsa then was building
a grand, new junior high school for the blacks.
The namers of the school—all white—would favor
figures like Booker T., because they felt
no threat from him. Booker had held out hope
for help from whites in lifting up his people.
Members of later generations frowned
on Booker T.'s accommodating to
a white-ruled world. They may have been too hard
on one who'd spent nine years in slavery, and
built up a school from nothing where one word
or move not carefully considered might
have left him hanging from the nearest tree.
Some critics wrote that George Washington Carver
"out-Bookered Booker," thus dismissing him.
George Carver's gentleness and feminine voice
made him appear too meek to be a hero,
especially the warrior kind, who tells
the white man, "Stop! We'll not be ruled by you."

*Booker T.
Washington*

Carver could not have been that kind of man.
He was, as Harry wrote, a prophet, seer,
which in the ancient, pre-political view
lives on the highest plane, beyond a warrior.
A soul like Carver's sees the widest vista
and works to delve into the deeper causes
inside, behind the things that meet his eyes.
The warrior is beyond the merchant, and
then laborers. Carver had played all these roles—
filling them well, with cheer and faith in God.
A man who campaigned hard to bring the day
when George's birthplace on old Mose's farm
became the Carver National Monument
said this of his inherent dignity:

> "This former slave has become a ruler in his own
> right in the empire of ideas, in the sphere of science...
> Most clearly he has seen how millions starve to death
> in a world that could live in peace and plenty on
> what it throws away."

The type of soul that Carver was—a man
who serves humanity free from all greed—
deserves to lead the people out of folly
with offerings of ideas freely drawn
from God. Honor is due to ones with wisdom.
Yet those who worship worldly wealth and power
have so obscured the ancient holy way
that on the earth, merchants of darkness reign.
Trapped so in self, they play the role of Cain.

The Tulsa School Board named the junior high
the George Washington Carver School. He went
with Harry Abbott for the dedication
in early May of 1929.
Again they stayed with Carlie and James Henry
and Carver early walked on Standpipe Hill
to study it in spring, in bud and bloom,

and greet anew his friends, God's multitudes
in all of nature's kingdoms.

Some people from the quieter towns and districts
called Tulsa "tush hog town." The urban centers
to them seemed too competitive and vicious.
By "tush hog"—from the Anglo-Saxon "tusk hog"—
they meant a man who lacked consideration
of others, and with habits coarse and loud.
If Tulsa had its vices, then to name
their junior high for George Washington Carver
was wise. He'd never tasted alcohol;
he'd seen it taking people—as he phrased it—
"out of the group of human beings." Carver
had never smoked. He called it suicide.
He never cursed or swore. He likely was
a lifelong celibate. Beyond these things,
he always could be counted on to love,
encourage, build and strengthen everyone.
He was a warrior of the Spirit's flame,
unwavering, with divinely guided sight,
while nature kept him flexible and light.

Relaxing near the Goodwins' door, he waited
one evening for a ride when Ed, the son

Thanks to Jeanne Goodwin.

*Edwin L.
Goodwin,
Sr., left, and
his father
James Henry
in the early
1950's.*

Jeanne Goodwin, three years after she met Carver.

Thanks to Jeanne Goodwin.

of James and Carlie, and his wife, named Jeanne,
dropped by from next door, where they had just moved.
Ed then worked with his dad in real estate
and later ran the *Oklahoma Eagle*,
Tulsa's black newspaper, for forty years.
Jeanne taught a class of elementary students
at Booker T., a thriving school that went
on through high school. In 1995,
when she was ninety-two, she called to mind
her memories of that meeting:

> "He didn't make you feel you were bothering him. It
> was in his nature to be courteous. But you knew he
> had better things to do than small talk. It was like he
> was in another world, looking forward or searching.

> "He wasn't begging for conversation. He didn't come
> in and say, 'How are you doing, blah, blah.' He did
> not initiate conversation, but he was receptive to
> anything anyone wanted to talk about. He heard your
> words and blended incoming knowledge with that
> which he already had."

Ed asked him if he planned to leave behind
his scientific secrets to his students.

His answer, spoken quietly, was, "No,
God will reveal to them the things they need."
He never left a list of formulae
for peanut products, knowing if he did
it would distract from his essential message:
Whatever we may need, at any moment,
we may discover, if we only learn
to tune in to the place where Jesus said
that heaven's kingdom is—within ourselves.
This was the message Carver wrote among
the autographs Jeanne was collecting, as
he quoted from the Bible Book of Proverbs:
> "In all thy ways acknowledge him, and he shall direct
> thy paths."

Jeanne said of Carver's clearly spiritual presence:
> "His mind was so far above mundane things and
> appearances that you would hardly notice his body.
> He was there but he wasn't there. He had an
> A-U-R-A about him. It was almost as if he didn't
> have a self. He seemed insulated against the world."

The meek and gentle Carver, when he saw
the Carver School's magnificence, felt awe.
He said it made him feel unworthy—more
than any honor he'd received before.

Three thousand, black and white, arrived to hear
his speech outdoors on temporary bleachers.
The street was closed and ceremoniously
some Boy Scouts raised the flag. A speaker stepped
up to the microphone—his old friend Penney,
the man who'd known him longest, since the days
at Agriculture School in Iowa.
Penney then told his story of the contest
in oratory, which George Carver won.
Penney's own speaking style, just five years later
would help convince the Tulsa voters to

elect him as their mayor, widely liked.
The second speaker was Principal Woods
who had with Mr. Hughes escorted Carver
two years before, to meet the all-white School Board
and watched him raise them past their thoughts of race.
Next Dr. Claxton, still the superintendent,
came forth to introduce the honoree.
The new school's namesake, George Washington Carver,
then slowly moved toward the microphone,
a new contraption that he hardly needed,
and said:

> "Ladies and Gentlemen, I trust you will pardon me
> for leaving off all preliminaries such as the telling of
> how glad I am to be here, my gratefulness to the Board
> of Education, Trustees and all others who contributed
> in any way toward making this occasion possible.
> Indeed I could spend the entire time at this, but I
> must not. Suffice it to say, that it is very apparent
> that some great, constructive, dynamic thinking
> personalities have been at work.

> "In this splendid building I see, to me, an exact
> interpretation of the following passages in Holy Writ.

> "I trust you will not be alarmed. I shall not attempt
> to preach a sermon; I shall do just as the average
> minister does—announce the texts, and depart from
> them, never to return."

He gave them a collection from the Bible
of words on vision, knowledge, and assurance,
and finally intoned a verse from Psalms—
an invocational prayer he often used
for tuning in to God:

> "'Open Thou mine eyes, O God, that I might behold
> the wondrous things.'"

In later speeches, he would illustrate
that prayer's importance with an incident
occurring in the Goodwins' living room.
Its light-blue walls, gold-flecked, suggested skies

of day; its chandelier the stars at night.

Carver was sitting near a radio,
then not a common sight and then quite large,
in fancy cabinets of wood, to hold
the space-consuming tubes. As he would tell it:

> "Once when I was in Tulsa, Oklahoma, my hostess
> on leaving the room said, 'There is the radio. If you
> like music just tune in.' When she returned I was
> sitting where she had left me. 'Why didn't you get
> some music?' she asked. 'I didn't know how to tune
> in,' I had to reply.

> "Do you know that is the trouble with many of us?
> And why we don't get on further and faster than we
> do? We don't know how to tune in, we don't know
> how to get in touch with educational forces or forces
> from which we wish to get information. There was
> nothing wrong with the radio or with the station,
> nor was there anything wrong with the air. I did not
> know how to tune in, therefore I got nothing.

> "If we are to talk with the Great Creator we must
> tune in. That little prayer was the final dial to put
> me in touch with Him."

Then Carver to the throng of Tulsa folks
both old and young spoke words out of his heart:

> "From the very beginning I have been greatly puzzled
> as to why this magnificent building should be named
> after me. Indeed why any building or anything should
> bear my name, when I, me, etc., represent such little
> things. To ease my mind I consulted the dictionary,
> and there I found the solution. This magnificent
> structure is not named after me, it is named after a
> great dynamic, constructive principle, and I happily
> bear that name. 'Carve' means to cut out, to fashion,
> to succeed, regardless of opposing forces. May God
> help each boy and girl, man and woman to catch the
> vision of a new day in opportunity, as set forth in
> this splendid building and its matchless equipment,
> for indeed each one is the architect of his own
> fortune, the carver of his own destiny."

So meditating on the name he'd taken
when he was ten—when Mrs. Watkins said
he'd need another name than "Carver's George,"
his old slave name, to register for school—
he made a point he hoped would help the youths
in Carver Junior High and all who came
to hear him speak: We each determine how
our lives proceed, by choices that we make.
The power of God available to us
is limitless. We only need to stay
tuned in, remembering: Our selves are small
and ultimately nothing—passing on
through form and phase through which we may express
the One beyond all things, the Infinite.

George Carver, ever wide awake within,
and studying the face of nature for
the Spirit in all things, was qualified
to say that mastery of destiny—
despite appearances—resides in us.
Glenn Clark, a friend to Carver, wrote of him:
   "He was gentle of speech, sly of humor,
    He was humble, simple and wise;
    Born a slave, he faced life as a master,
    While his Master's light shone through his eyes."
Harry recalled of him:
   "...on our first trip to Tulsa, Oklahoma, the papers
   referred to him as botanist, chemist, agriculturist, and
   research scientist. On our return I said to him, 'Dr.
   Carver, they call you so many things, just what are
   you?' He replied in terse, simple language, 'I am a
   master of things.' Then he explained to me that when
   he set himself to a task he mastered every necessary
   operation and sought every bit of available
   information. If he needed botany, chemistry, physics,
   mathematics, or even music as an aid or means, he
   employed any or all of them; and if he did not have

them, he got them. Time after time I have heard him
tell audiences of young people to learn all they could
about things around them—the trees, flowers, weeds,
birds..."

What George Washington Carver told the young
he said to all: "Search nature for your God.
Become a master and a useful servant
in lifting of the suffering you find."
Some folks believe salvation is so big
they must do great grand acts to bring it in.
George Carver knew that every little thing
we do and say will help or hurt the world.
The wisdom which true science helps provide
comes by such simple steps. God be your guide!

THANKS!

Jeanne Goodwin, God be with you! and your friends:
Pal Coleman, Jobie Holderness, Ruth Avery,
Jewel Proctor Hines and Ms. Eddie Faye Gates—
so thoughtful, helpful, free with offerings
of useful information.
And thank you Robert Powers and Jeff Kauffman
of the historical society
in Tulsa, answering my called-in questions
with patient kindness. Thanks so much Paul Buck!
devoted botanist and generous scholar,
for taking me—as you all have—to Tulsa
before I could afford to visit you
in person, through accounts and listening
to what I wrote to check it for its truth.
Thanks *Oklahoma Eagle*! May you prosper
for good work serving your community
and for the space you gave me when you ran
an early draft of this.

Thanks Dad for spurring me to start this, and
for faith in me, and patient understanding.
Thanks Mom for love. Thank you, Ed Brian, for
your stringless risk of money for the printing
and friendship shared as you have listened to
my Shakespeare readings, solely for the joy.
Dear Norah Porter who has passed the way
to happiness in heaven, leaving me
a place to keep on working, rest in peace!
This work holds your encouragement and cheer.
Burr Overstreet, your unassuming nature
has left me free to work and make great progress
on all our camping travels.

Thanks Lucy Despard: Using your kind gift
I took a research trip, enabling me
to find most of the photos in this book.
Thank God for libraries! and for those souls
so helpful who work in them. For example
Marisa Bowen at the Civic Center,
showing a kindly interest in this project.
John Sides, you've kept a poor man's old computer
continually revived through hard drive crashes
all out of love for Carver and this work.
The Powells, Jack and Jessica, dear friends,
thanks for your scanning, faxing, and your readings!
Arisa Victor, thanks for checking text,
and Jean McMann for balanced commentary
and sister Lee for fruitful listening.
And Dr. Daniel Williams of Tuskegee
has shown unfailing generosity
in sharing Carver's legacy with me.
The Pennunuris, Ralph and Beth, thanks for
the "cherry on the top," the final title.

Kate Henke, you have been a godsend! Thanks!
Your kind receptive competence and time
have made this book's appearance possible.
Thank you my sunny love Teresa Ashby,
my "final editor" and soulful mate.
God bless you all, you kind encouragers!
My work is done on waves of your uplifting.

A NOTE FROM
P. D. BURCHARD TO THE READER

In seeking souls whose teachings help dispel
the ignorance behind our suffering,
I've searched the scriptures, which give power to sift
the truth from lies. They helped me recognize
in Carver, one who spoke the truth from God.
When, almost ten years back, my dad called up
to offer me an opportunity
to write a volume for a series of
American biographies (although
this later grew to something else), I knew
that if I was to spend a year or two
(which seemed enough) focusing on a person,
I wanted one who still would be my teacher—
whose words would always lift me toward the light.
George Carver, though he had his little foibles,
has never let me down.
Like most, I'd only known of Carver as
the Peanut Man. Then, in the nineteen seventies
I found in Glenn Clark's book a portrait of
a great exalted spirit.
Carver, knowing that God is love, would sweep
all thoughts of hate effortlessly away.
Among his many loving letters is
this summary of thoughts on hate and love:
> "Hate, my dear friend, is the very embodiment of
> everything that is wrong. Nothing too revolting or
> destructive for it to do; turns us into fiends incarnate.

> "Love is divine, is of God, must some day rule the
> world. It is the only force that has held the world
> together up to date. When we cease to love our fellow
> men, we have become a dangerous character because
> we have shut God (love) out of our lives."

My own forbears sailed from the shores of Europe.
This means, as students of genetics know,
that, like all Europeans, I'm a hybrid—

being one-third African, the rest from Asia.
Real science, free of blinding biases,
can teach us that, to God and nature, "race"
has no reality. It is a name
that ignorance has hung on differences
too superficial to take seriously.
The differences between two individuals
are greater, far, genetically, than those
which stir up prejudice in folks who hate.
That ancient burden which we've labeled "race"
is on this country's mind continually,
so unresolved. I grew up in the North,
where "whites" could think our minds were freer than
they were because the segregation was
more subtle than the blatant Southern setup—
though just as real, veiled by hypocrisy—
enabling people to avoid the truth
that shallow smiles hid thoughts less kind and free.

The truth that sees through lies is at its best
when resting on the affirmation of
the way things really are.
In Carver's words, I hear such stable truth:
   "God, my beloved friend, is infinite, the highest
   embodiment of love. We are finite, surrounded and
   often filled with hate. We can only understand the
   infinite as we loose the finite and take on the
   infinite."

A spirit of such breadth is sure to leave
a student of his with a heightened vision—
helping to lift our self-burdened but hopeful species,
so often using powers in ignorance,
beyond these desperate times.

Peter Duncan Burchard
Fairfax, California
January, 1998

SOURCES

Books

Clark, Glenn, *The Man Who Talks With the Flowers*, St. Paul, Minnesota: Macalester Park Publishing Co., 1939. This book is still in publication, by the same company.

Elliott, Lawrence: *George Washington Carver, The Man Who Overcame*, Englewood Cliffs, New Jersey: Prentice-Hall, Inc., 1966.

Ellsworth, Scott, *Death In a Promised Land*, Baton Rouge, Louisiana and London: Louisiana State University Press, 1982. Thanks to Jeanne Goodwin for sending this book to me.

Franks, Kenny A., *You're Doin' Fine, Oklahoma!*, Oklahoma City: Diamond Jubilee Commission, Oklahoma Historical Society, 1983. Thanks to Jeanne Goodwin for sending this book to me.

Imes, Dr. G. Lake, *I Knew Carver* (no more information available).

Kremer, Gary, *George Washington Carver: In His Own Words*, Columbia, Missouri: University of Missouri Press, 1987.

Little, Mabel, with Hare, Nathan, Ph.D., and Hare, Julia, Ph.D., *Fire on Mount Zion: My Life and History as a Black Woman in America*, Langston, Oklahoma: Langston University and Black Think Tank, 1990. Thanks to Jeanne Goodwin for sending this book to me.

Means, Florence Crannel, *Carver's George*, Boston, Massachusetts: Houghton Mifflin Company, 1952.

Miller, Basil, *George Washington Carver, God's Ebony Scientist*, Grand Rapids, Michigan: Zondervan Publishing House, 1943.

Smith, Alvin D., *George Washington Carver, Man of God*, New York: Exposition Press, 1954.

Archives

Lucy Cherry Crisp Papers (in notes as LCC) at East Carolina University, Greenville, North Carolina.

Tuskegee Institute Archives (in notes as TIA) at Tuskegee University, Tuskegee, Alabama; George Washington Carver Papers. Microfilm references from these papers are written with reel number followed by frame number, as 63, 865.

NOTES

p. 2: train stop in Neosho: Carver to Mrs. Goodwin of Neosho, 12/28/28, George Washington Carver National Monument, catalog #1389; printed in Kremer, 39-40.

p. 5: George's clothes and possessions: Lucy Cherry Crisp interview of Carver, June 1934; LCC, 154.20h.

p. 5-6:description of Aunt Mariah: interview by Jessie P. Guzman of Tuskegee with Mrs. Mary Cuther; TIA, 63, 865.

p. 6: Cal Jefferson quote: Jessie P. Guzman interview in Granby, Missouri, 5/28/48; TIA 63, 664.

p. 7: Tulsa history: largely from Ellsworth, p. 8-11.

p. 8: Carver to Harry Abbott, Chicago, Illinois: 5/1/33; TIA, 14, 443; original held by Carver National Monument, Diamond, Missouri. I have left quotes of Carver's as he wrote them with the exception of this one because it contains an error which has no effect on the sense but would be jarringly distracting at this point in the narrative. The affected part of the original reads: "...seemed especially happy when you could add anything to my personal comfortable..." He once wrote: "I am more interested in the ideas expressed than the mechanics of writing."

p. 9: Harry Abbott, Chicago, Illinois, to Carver: 12/31/39; TIA, 32, 348.

p. 9: Mr. Hooker meeting Carver's train: Harry Abbott to Robert Russa Moton, President of Tuskegee Institute, a report on the trip, 10/12/27; TIA, 48, 689.

p. 9: Mr. Hooker's business partnership: interview (all interviews for this book were by telephone) of 12/8/95 with Jeanne Goodwin, James Henry and Carlie's daughter-in-law, whose great generosity and belief in this work has been of immeasurable importance.

p. 11: "If you want to see fine clothes...": Means, p. 155-6.

p. 11: "I don't know how I look...": Carver to Georgia Cummings, St. Petersburg, Florida, 4/27/42; TIA, 40, 1155.

p. 11-13: description of the Goodwins and their house: interview with Jeanne Goodwin, 8/4/95.

p. 13: informed of Superintendent's invitation: Harry Abbott to Robert Russa Moton, 10/12/27; TIA, 48, 690.

p. 14: Goodwins' sojourn to Tulsa: interview with Jeanne Goodwin, 7/27/95.

p. 14: Pennsylvania oilmen: interview with Ruth Avery, 12/9/95.

p. 15: weather of 10/5/27 (and throughout book): from weather reports in the *Tulsa World*, located by Delbert Amen of the Oklahoma Historical Society.

p. 16: trees by river, and Creek tribe: interview with Robert Powers of the Tulsa Historical Society, September 1995. Mr. Powers and his co-worker Jeff Kauffman have been invaluable resources.

p. 16: Tulsa's celebration of statehood (11/16/07): from Franks.

p. 16-17:theft of land from Indians: interview with Jeanne Goodwin, 7/27/95.

p. 17: Carver on heaven and hell: Smith, p. 27-8.

p. 18: Carver on ores and oil: Elliott, p. 208. Permission to use quote granted from Simon and Schuster.

p. 20: Carver and Abbott at fairgrounds: Harry Abbott to Robert Russa Moton, 10/12/27; TIA, 48, 689.

p. 20: description of fairgrounds, here and on p. 28 (barkers, projects youth had made): "Negroes Ready to Open Great Fair at 1:30 Wednesday," *Tulsa Tribune* 10/4/27 and "Negro State Fair Offers Variety of Extra Features," *Tulsa Tribune*, 10/6/27. Thanks to Paul Buck, Professor Emeritus in Botany at the University of Tulsa. I contacted him for botanical information and he went to the trouble to search out these articles which included much material on the fair. Thanks to Paralee Coleman for her firsthand account, providing rich details.

p. 20-22: Carver and Abbott on Standpipe Hill: Harry Abbott to Robert Russa Moton, 10/12/27; TIA, 48, 689-90.

p. 20: Standpipe Hill: interview with Jeanne Goodwin, 7/3/95.

p. 21-22 & 24: Standpipe Hill's geology and botany, and its present state: Paul Buck to the author, 8/15/95, a letter including an account of inquiries and a field trip he made especially to aid this work, along with photocopied information on the local geology.

p. 22: Carver on windows: Carver to Hubert W. Peet, 2/24/30, manuscript enclosed with a letter; TIA, 12, 31; published in *World Friends* magazine, May 1932; TIA, 46, 820.

p. 23-24: Harry Abbott on stopping by the road: from transcript of a radio show recorded soon after Carver's death; statement read by Tom Campbell at Tuskegee from a letter from Harry Abbott; TIA, 63, 409.

p. 25: Klan crosses up on Standpipe Hill: interview with Jeanne Goodwin, 7/27/95.

p. 25: brick plant: interviews with Jeanne Goodwin, 7/3/95 and Robert Powers, 8/1/95.

p. 25: "Begin at once to study...": Carver to Theodore Hall, Emory, Virginia, 11/21/26; TIA, 46, 1132.

p. 26: "I do love the things...": Carver to James T. Hardwick, Blacksburg, Virginia, 5/21/24; TIA, 7, 1163.

p. 26: return to fair grounds: Harry Abbott to Robert Russa Moton, 10/12/27; TIA, 48, 690.

p. 26: "What the opening hours...": *Tulsa Tribune*, 10/6/27.

p. 26: description of Penney: interview with Ruth Avery, 12/9/95.

p. 26-27:Carver's talk with T. A. Penney: Harry Abbott to Robert Russa Moton, 10/12/27; TIA, 48, 690.

p. 27: oratorical contest story: Little, Hare, and Hare, p. 81.

p. 27-28: entrance to fair free; poultry: *Tulsa Tribune*, 10/6/27.

p. 28: Negro Wall Street, Monte Carlo: Ellsworth, p. 15.

p. 28: northern section so alive: interview with Jeanne Goodwin, December, 1995.

p. 28: Indians at fair: interview with Paralee Coleman, 8/14/95.

p. 28: "We especially invite...": *Tulsa Tribune*, 10/4/27.

p. 30, 33 & 35: Carver's meeting with School Board: Harry Abbott to Robert Russa Moton, 10/12/27; 48, 690.

p. 30: description of Principals Hughes and Woods: interview with Jeanne Goodwin, December, 1995.

p. 30: anomalous, unusual: interviews, respectively, with Robert Powers, 8/1/95 and Ruth Avery, 12/9/95.

p. 30-32: riot: Ellsworth, p. 47; interview with Ruth Avery, 12/9/95.

p. 31: "If I knew you...": Carver to Mr. Dana Storm, Los Angeles, California, 6/19/42; TIA, 41, 853.

p. 33: description of Superintendent Claxton: interview with Ruth Avery, 12/9/95.

p. 34: "there is no question or questions...": typed transcript of speech of 1/29/13; TIA 46, 880.

p. 35: "I have had some very unusual...": 5/20/29; TIA, 11, 926.

p. 35: "In my opinion Dr. Carver's...": Harry Abbott to Robert Russa Moton, 10/12/27; 48, 692.

p. 35: "I put off the finite...": Lillian R. Rowan, Wichita, Kansas, to Carver, recounting her meeting with him, 10/2/42; TIA, 43, 80.

p. 35-36: Dunbar school visit, "using Dr. Carver as...": Harry Abbott to Robert Russa Moton, 10/12/27; TIA, 48, 691.

p. 36: Jobie Holderness and the future minister: interview with Jobie Holderness, 2/4/96.

p. 38: students taking home plants: interview with Jeanne Goodwin, December, 1995.

p. 38: Tuskegee song (second verse, second half): TIA, 67 [a], 392.

p. 38: "Because I've loved...": quoted in Sullivan, Leo, Producer, Paul Laurence Dunbar, Vignette Films, 1966.

p. 38: fair Friday: Harry Abbott to Robert Russa Moton, 10/12/27; TIA, 48, 691.

p. 38-41: Paralee Coleman: interview with Paralee "Pal" Coleman, 7/6/95.

p. 41: Will Rogers visit to Tuskegee: Imes; TIA, 59, 1070.

p. 41: Rogers' words to Carver: J. W. Holly, President of Georgia Normal and Industrial School for Young Colored Men and Women, to Carver, 3/14/28; TIA, 10, 1136.

p. 41: Carver's Friday night meeting: Harry Abbott to Robert Russa Moton, 10/12/27; TIA, 48, 691.

p. 43: description of crowd: interview with Ed Goodwin, Jr., 6/30/95, and Paralee Coleman, 7/13/95.

p. 43: obstructions by whites to rebuilding of North Tulsa: Ellsworth, p. 85-7.

p. 43: building back up of North Tulsa: interviews with Jeff Kauffman, Tulsa Historical Society, June 1995, and Ed Goodwin, Jr., 6/30/95.

p. 43: couldn't try a hat on: interviews with Jeanne Goodwin 7/27/95 and Paralee Coleman 8/1/95.

p. 44-52: all quotes from Friday night meeting: "Finds Rubber Forest in Tulsa," Black Dispatch, 10/13/27. Thanks to Delbert Amen of the Oklahoma Historical Society, who sent me a copy of this speech, of which I was missing a part. I had asked him for weather reports for Carver's time in Tulsa and "anything else you might find on his trip," and he gave me this extra boost which has made a huge difference!

p. 45: photo caption: Ovington, Mary White, Portraits in Color,

New York: The Viking Press, date not available, p. 170.

p. 45: hydrocarbons, carbohydrates: Thanks to John Roulac of Hemptech, Ojai, California, for sending me a copy of his book *Industrial Hemp*, containing this information. Roulac's book is printed on paper made of hemp, a plant which Carver admired for its wonderful fiber.

p. 46: "I found him wandering...": Jessie P. Guzman interview with Mr. O. L. Lennen, Ness City, Kansas 1948; TIA, 63, 651.

p. 47: photo of Roscoe Dunjee: printed in Teall, Kaye M., ed., *Black History in Oklahoma: A Resource Book,* Oklahoma City: Oklahoma City Public Schools, 1971.

p. 48: Roscoe Dunjee, Oklahoma City, Oklahoma, to Carver: 2/2/36; TIA, 18, 822.

p. 50: back-to-the-farm movement: Little, Hare, and Hare, p. 94.

p. 51: Thomas Edison's request for students: Edison to Carver 5/27/27; TIA, 10, 674. The message was sent by "Ediphone," a dictating machine with a device for entering corrections automatically.

p. 52-54: refinery visit: Harry Abbott to Robert Russa Moton, 10/12/27; TIA, 48, 691-2.

p. 52-54: description of refinery: interview with Robert Powers, Tulsa Historical Society, 6/22/95.

p. 53: alcohol fuel: interview with John Roulac of Hemptech, Ojai, California, July, 1995.

p. 53: products of refinery: "Negro Scientist to Seek Uses for Refinery Refuse," *Tulsa Tribune*, 10/9/27: 2D. Thanks to Delbert Amen of the Oklahoma Historical Society for finding this article for me.

p. 54: "the type of life...": Carver to Mrs. Katherine E. Williamson, Mt. Vernon, New York, 2/28/41; TIA, 36, 703.

p. 54: sludge holding ponds: interview with Jeff Kauffman, Tulsa Historical Society, September, 1995.

p. 55-56: geological information: interview with Alan Benison of Tulsa, 9/23/95.

p. 56: sludge: Carver to W. F. Graham, 11/15/27 (just received jar of sludge); TIA, 10, 870; H. T. Bennett to Carver, 12/15/27; TIA, 10, 950; Carver to H. T. Bennett, 12/20/27; TIA, 10, 961.

p. 56: Mid-Continent asphaltines: Thanks to Jim Leonard of San Rafael, California, for finding this information.

p. 57: always sleep over a problem: Miller, p. 122.

p. 57: photo caption: source information unavailable on clipping from which this was copied

p.56-58: W. F. Graham, Business Manager, Tulsa Board of Education, to Carver, 11/4/27; TIA, 10, 858; Graham to Carver, 3/5/28; TIA, 10, 1110; Carver to Graham 3/14/28; TIA, 10, 1133.

p. 60: "This former slave...": Richard Pilant, St. Louis, Missoui to Carver 7/15/42, eulogistic statement enclosed with a note; TIA, 42, 235.

p.61: definition of "tush hog town": interviews with Jeanne Goodwin, 7/3/95 and 7/23/95, and Paralee Coleman, 7/13/95.

p. 61-63: meeting of Ed and Jeanne Goodwin with Carver: interviews with Jeanne Goodwin, December, 1995 and July, 1996.

p. 62-63:Jeanne Goodwin's observations on Carver: interviews of (in order of use) 7/1/95, 7/23/95, 7/28/95, 8/4/95, 7/2/95, and 9/14/95.

p. 63: felt unworthy: Carver to Judge Leon McCord, Montgomery, Alabama, 5/15/29; TIA, 11, 903.

p. 64: crowd and ceremony at dedication exercises: "George W. Carver Speaker at Negro School Dedication," *Tulsa Tribune*, 5/5/29: D1, column 2; "Dedicate Negro Jr. High School," *Tulsa World*, 5/6/29, p. 4, column 5. Thanks to Delbert Amen of the Oklahoma Historical Society for finding these articles for me.

p. 64-65: Carver's speech at dedication: from a typed transcript; TIA, 46, 933-4.

The Bible verses Carver quoted, listed in the transcript, are a collection of his often-repeated favorites:

Under the heading "Vision": "Where there is no vision, the people perish." (Proverbs 29:18); "Your young men shall see visions and your old men shall dream dreams." (Joel 2:28).

Under "Knowledge": "For the earth shall be filled with the knowledge of the glory of the Lord, as the waters covered the sea." (Habakkuk 2:14); "Behold, I have given you every herb that bears seed upon the face of the earth, and every tree bearing seed. To you it shall be for meat." (Genesis 1:29); "There is much food in the tillage of the poor, but there is that is wasted through want of judg-ment." (Proverbs 13:23); The heavens declare the glory of God, and the earth showeth forth His handiwork." (Psalms 19:1).

Under "Assurance": "God moves in a mysterious way His wonders to perform." (Not from the Bible, though Carver thought it was. The line was written by the poet William Cowper.); "Behold, I shall shew you a mystery." (I Corinthians 15:51); "In all thy ways acknowledge him, and he shall direct thy paths." (Proverbs 3:6).

p. 64-65: radio metaphor: Harry Abbott to Carver, 11/28/38; TIA, 26, 826 (incident mentioned); interview with Jeanne Goodwin, 9/14/95 (location of radio); "An Evening with the Creative Mind," *The Tuskegee Messenger*, May 1934, v. 10, #5, p. 6; TIA, 46, 829 (Carver's speech).

p. 66: Glenn Clark's poem on Carver: Clark, p. 61.

p. 67: Harry Abbott on "master of things": from transcript of a radio show recorded soon after Carver's death; statement read by Tom Campbell at Tuskegee from a letter from Harry Abbott; TIA, 63, 409.

p. 70: "Hate, my dear friend...": Carver to James T. Hardwick, Blacksburg, Virginia, 12/25/28; TIA, 11, 501.

p. 71: "That ancient burden...": I have borrowed the language of this sentence from the words of Mary Frances Berry in Lanker, Brian, *I Dream a World*, New York: Stewart, Tabori and Chang, 1989, p. 84.

p. 71: "God, my beloved...": Carver to Jack E. Boyd, Denver, Colorado, 3/1/27; TIA, 10, 636.

p. 73: "I am more interested...": Carver to Dana Johnson, Columbus, Georgia, 2/21/31, George Washington Carver National Monument, catalog #1705, quoted in Kremer, xii.

back cover: "I was expecting...": Frasier, Scottie McKenzie, in *The Dothan (Alabama) Eagle*, 1931? (year uncertain in microfilms); TIA, 61, 104.

back cover: "I am so glad...": Carver to James T. Hardwick, Blacksburg, Virginia, 11/26/28; TIA, 11, 429.